The 21st Century Guitar Method

GUITAR NECK

DIAGRAM BOOK

Autography by Rose Rottmayer
Project Managers: Aaron Stang and Colgan Bryan
Art Design: Joseph Klucar

Alfred Music Publishing Co., Inc.
16320 Roscoe Blvd., Suite 100
P.O. Box 10003
Van Nuys, CA 91410-0003
alfred.com

ISBN-10: 0-7692-9226-7
ISBN-13: 978-0-7692-9226-7

Music Notation

There are seven natural notes. They are named for the first seven letters of the alphabet: A B C D E F G. After G, we begin again with A.

Music is written on a **staff**. The staff consists of five lines with four spaces between the lines:

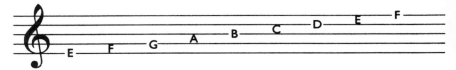

At the beginning of the staff is a treble or G clef. (The treble clef is known as the G clef because it encircles the 2nd line G.) The clef determines the location of notes on the staff. All guitar music is written on a treble clef.

The notes are written on the staff in alphabetical order. The first line is E:

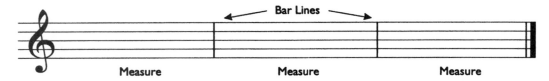

Notes can extend above, and below, the treble clef. When they do, **ledger lines** are added. Following is the approximate range of the guitar from the lowest note, open sixth string "E," to "B" on the first string, 17th fret.

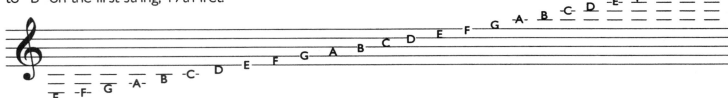

The staff is divided into **measures** by **bar lines**. A heavy double bar line marks the end of the music:

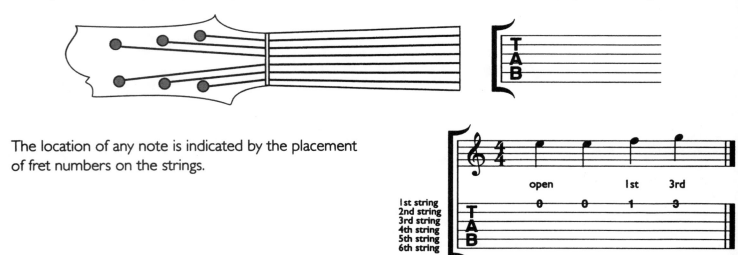

Tablature is a type of music notation that is specific to the guitar; its use dates back to the 1600s. Tablature illustrates the location of notes on the neck of the guitar. Tablature is usually used in conjunction with a music staff. The notes and rhythms are indicated in the music staff; the tablature shows where those notes are played on the guitar.

The location of any note is indicated by the placement of fret numbers on the strings.

Rhythm Notation and Time Signatures

At the beginning of every song is a time signature. 4/4 is the most common time signature:

4
4   FOUR COUNTS TO A MEASURE
    A QUARTER NOTE RECEIVES ONE COUNT

The top number tells you how many counts per measure.
The bottom number tells you which kind of note receives one count.

The time value of a note is determined by three things:

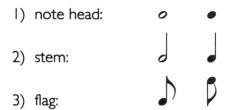

1) note head:

2) stem:

3) flag:

o This is a **whole note**. The note head is open and has no stem. In 4/4 time, a whole note receives 4 counts.

This is a **half note**. It has an open note head and a stem. A half note receives 2 counts.

This is a **quarter note**. It has a solid note head and a stem. A quarter note receives 1 count.

This is an **eighth note**. It has a solid note head and a stem with a flag attached. An eighth note receives 1/2 count.

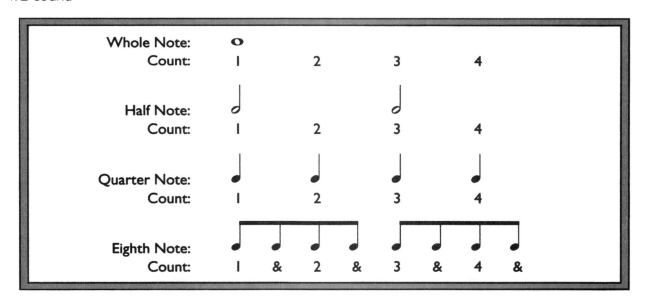

Whole Note:	o			
Count:	1	2	3	4
Half Note:	♩		♩	
Count:	1	2	3	4
Quarter Note:	♩	♩	♩	♩
Count:	1	2	3	4
Eighth Note:	♪♪	♪♪	♪♪	♪♪
Count:	1 &	2 &	3 &	4 &

Count out loud and clap the rhythm to this excerpt from "Jingle Bells."

Four counts per measure

Jin - gle bells!   Jin - gle bells!   Jin - gle all the way!
1   2   3   4   1   2   3   4   1   2   3   4   1   2   3   4

A quarter note receives one count

Chord Construction

All chords are built from the major scale. **You can figure out the notes in any major scale by applying this pattern of whole- and half-steps: W W H W W W H.** (A half-step is equal to the distance from one fret to the next, a whole-step is two frets.)

For example, the A major scale:

A	B	C#	D	E	F#	G#	A
W	W	H	W	W	W	H	

The scale tones can be numbered:

A	B	C#	D	E	F#	G#	A	B	C#	D	E	F#
1	2	3	4	5	6	7	8	9	10	11	12	13

Any chord can be built from its corresponding major scale by applying the appropriate chord pattern.

Chord Patterns		Examples (Key of A)	
Major:	1 3 5	A:	A C# E
Minor:	1 ♭3 5	Am:	A C E
Dominant 7:	1 3 5 ♭7	A7:	A C# E G
Major 7:	1 3 5 7	Amaj7:	A C# E G#
Major 6:	1 3 5 6	A6:	A C# E F#
Minor 7:	1 ♭3 5 ♭7	Am7:	A C E G
Add 9:	1 3 5 9	A(9):	A C# E B
Suspended 4:	1 4 5	Asus:	A D E
Dominant 9:	1 3 5 ♭7 9	A9:	A C# E G B
Dominant 13:	1 3 5 ♭7 13	A13:	A C# E G F#
Dominant 7(♭9):	1 3 5 ♭7 ♭9	A7(♭9):	A C# E G B♭
Minor 9:	1 ♭3 5 9	Am9:	A C E B
Minor 7(♭5):	1 ♭3 ♭5 ♭7	Am7(♭5):	A C E♭ G
Diminished 7:	1 ♭3 ♭5 ♭♭7*(6)	A°7:	A C E♭ F#
Augmented:	1 3 #5	A+:	A C# E#
Dominant 7(#5):	1 3 #5 ♭7	A7(#5):	A C# E# G
Dominant 7(#9):	1 3 5 ♭7 #9**(♭3)	A7(#9):	A C# E G C♮

* ♭♭7 = 6
** #9 = ♭3

How to Read Chord Frames

A chord frame is a diagram of the guitar neck.

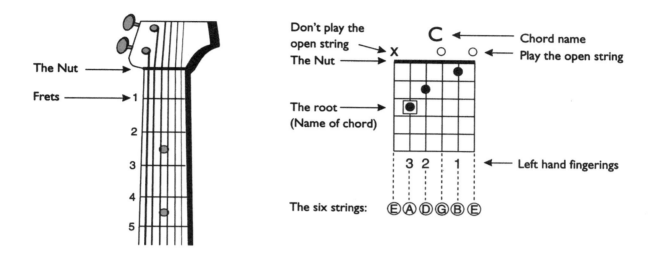

The location of chords played higher up the neck is indicated with a fret number.

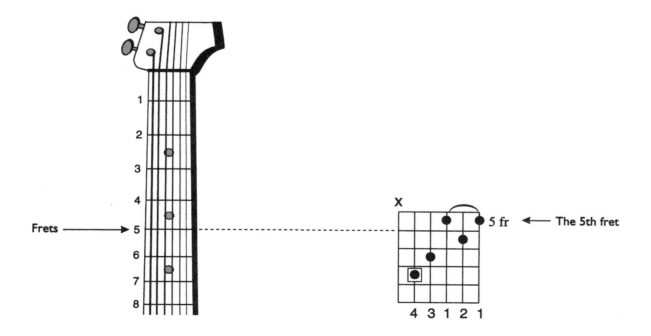

Guitar Chord Chart

The following chart shows all of the most commonly used guitar chords.
"o" indicates an open string. "x" indicates the string is not to be played.

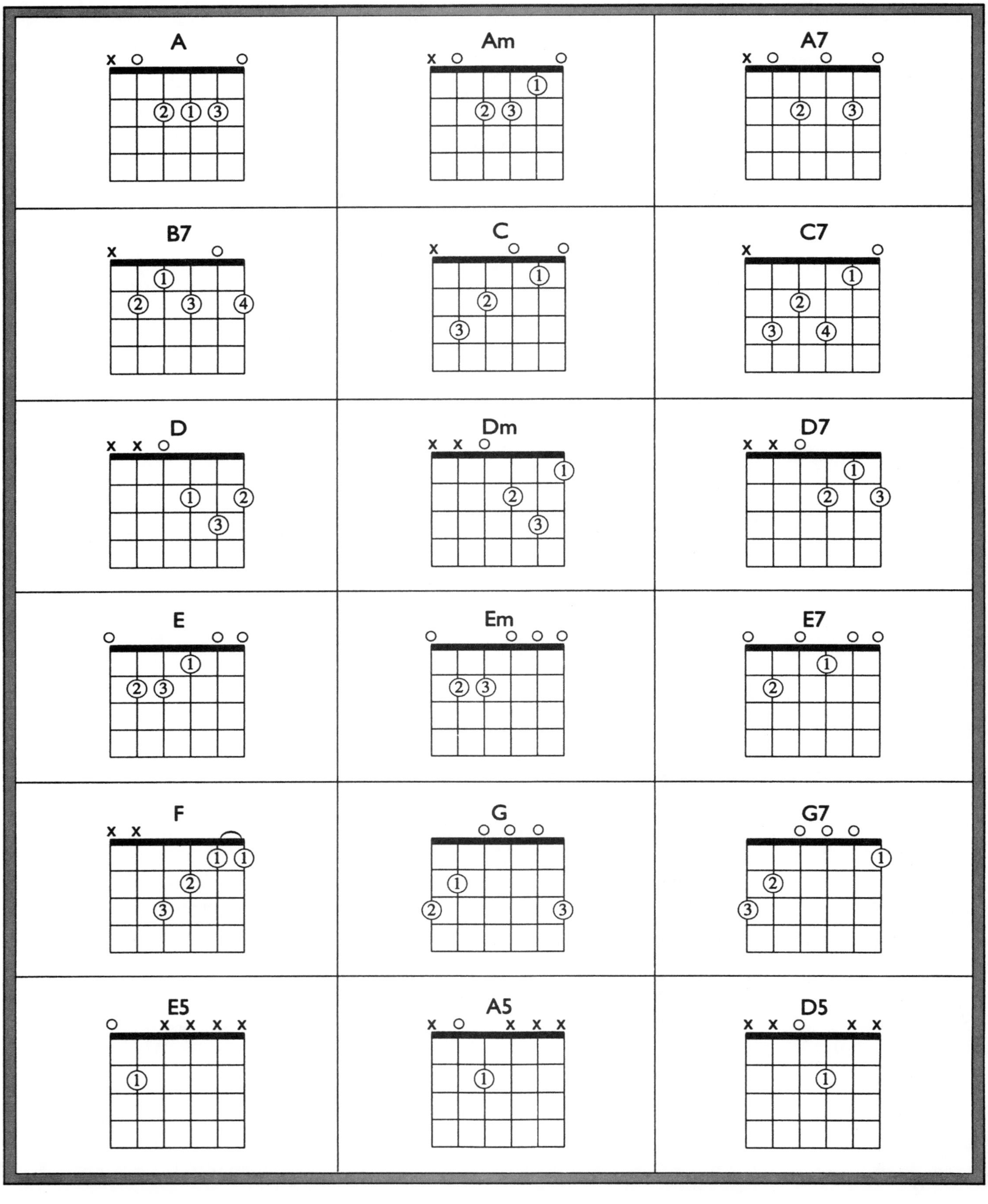

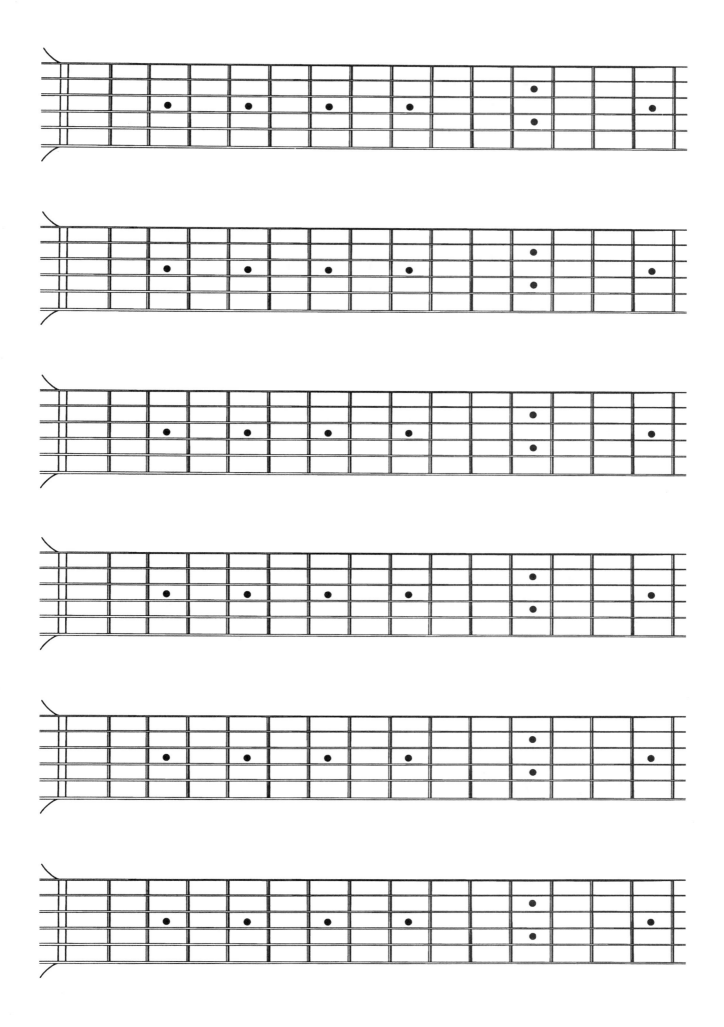

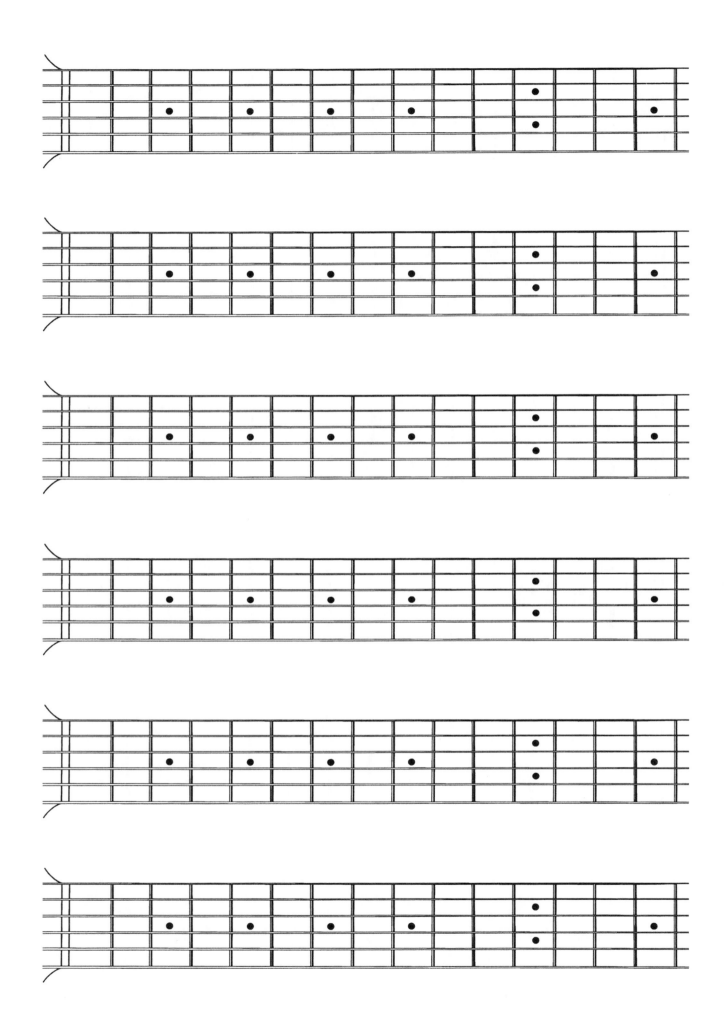

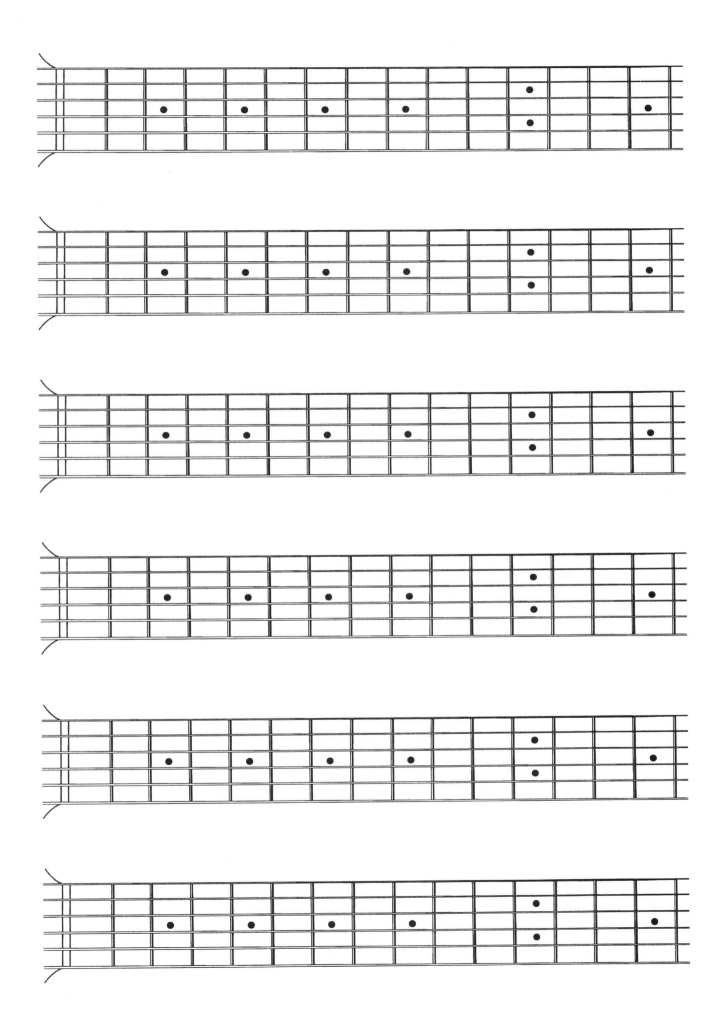

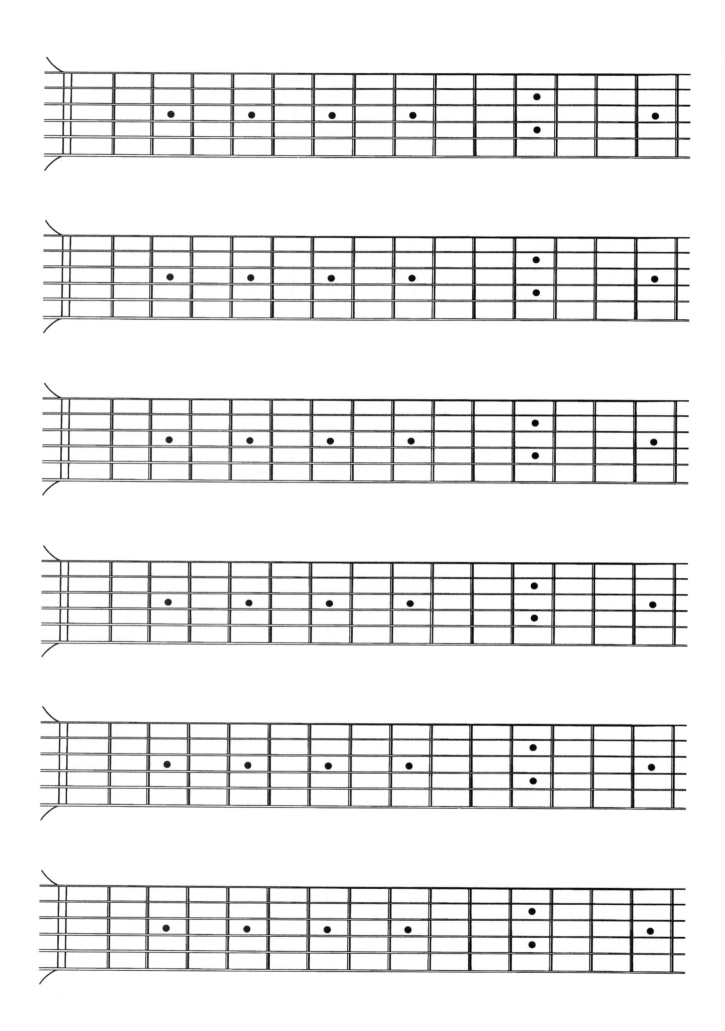

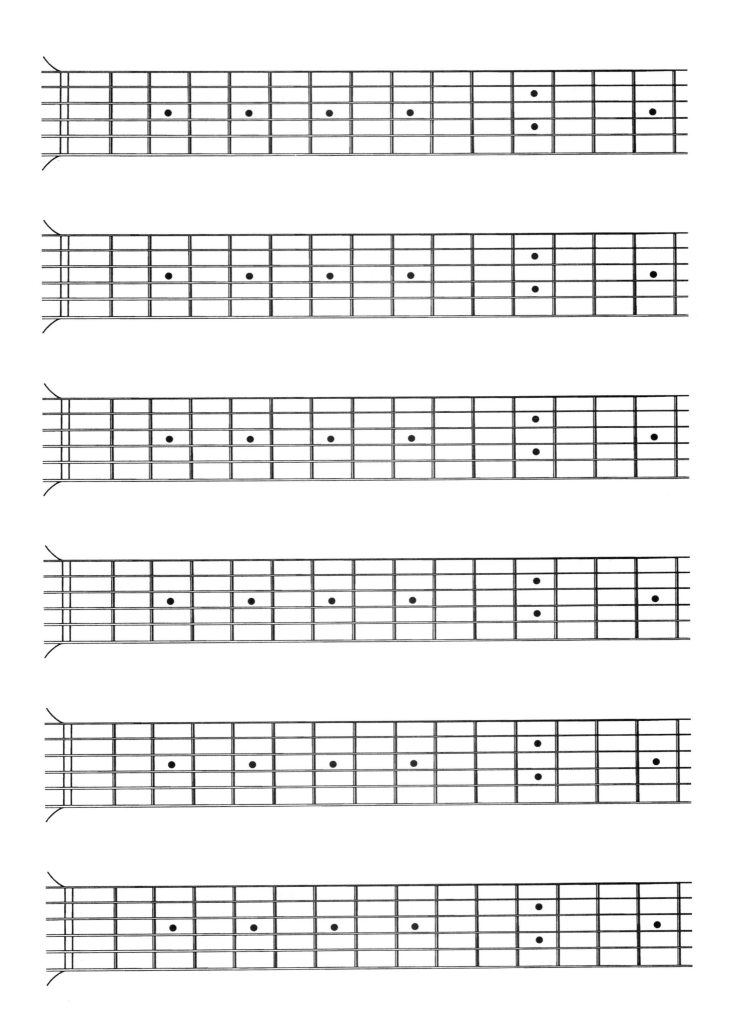

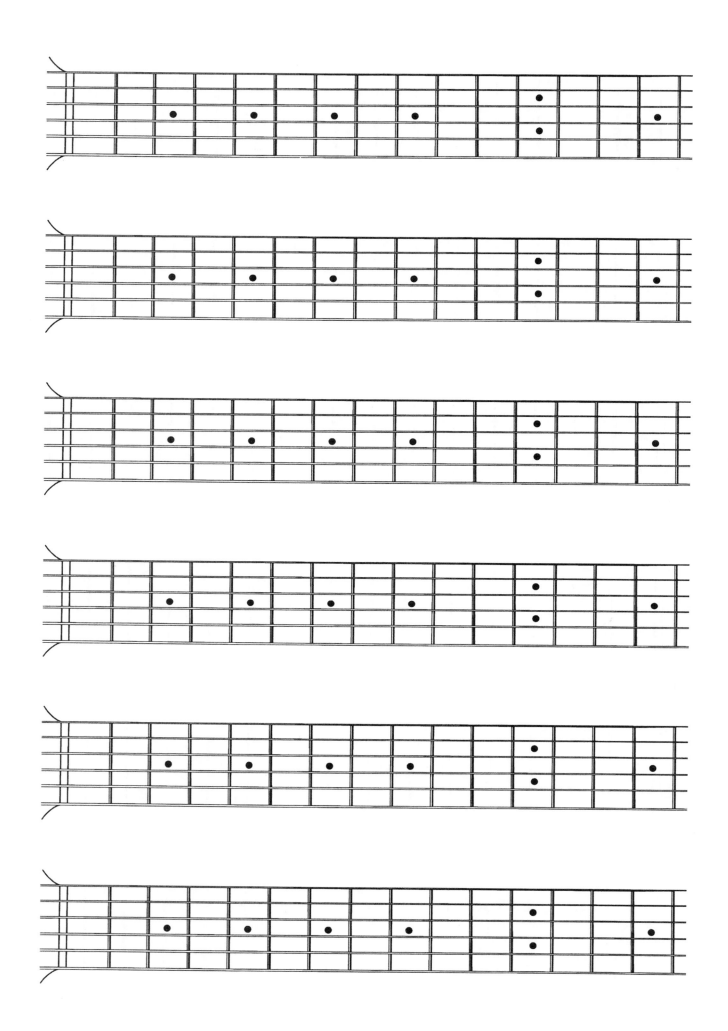

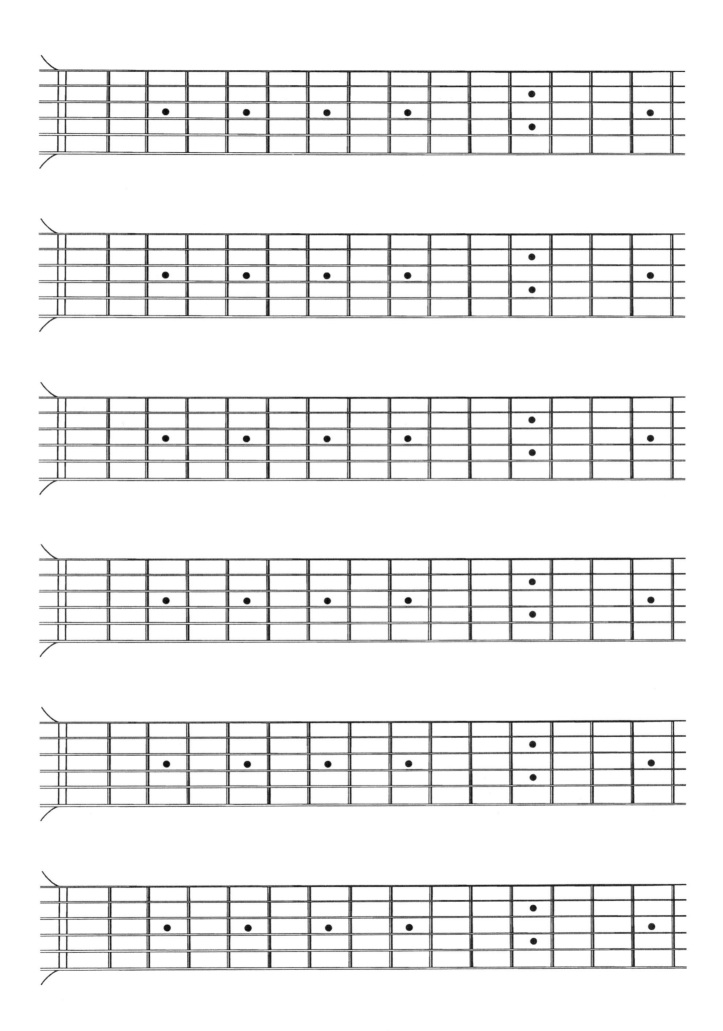

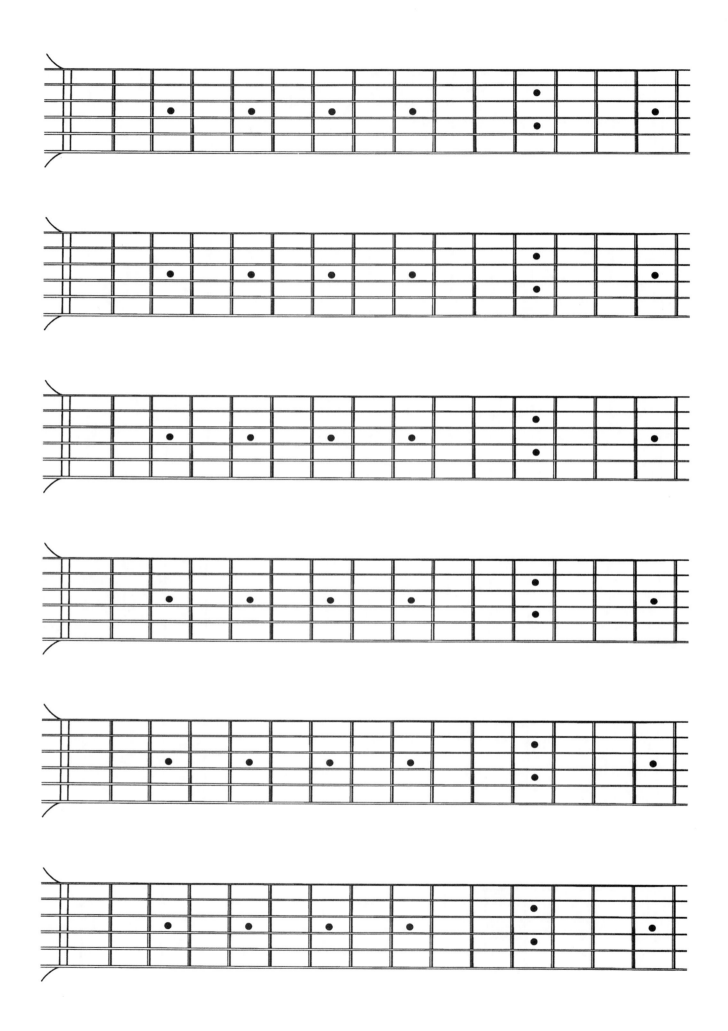

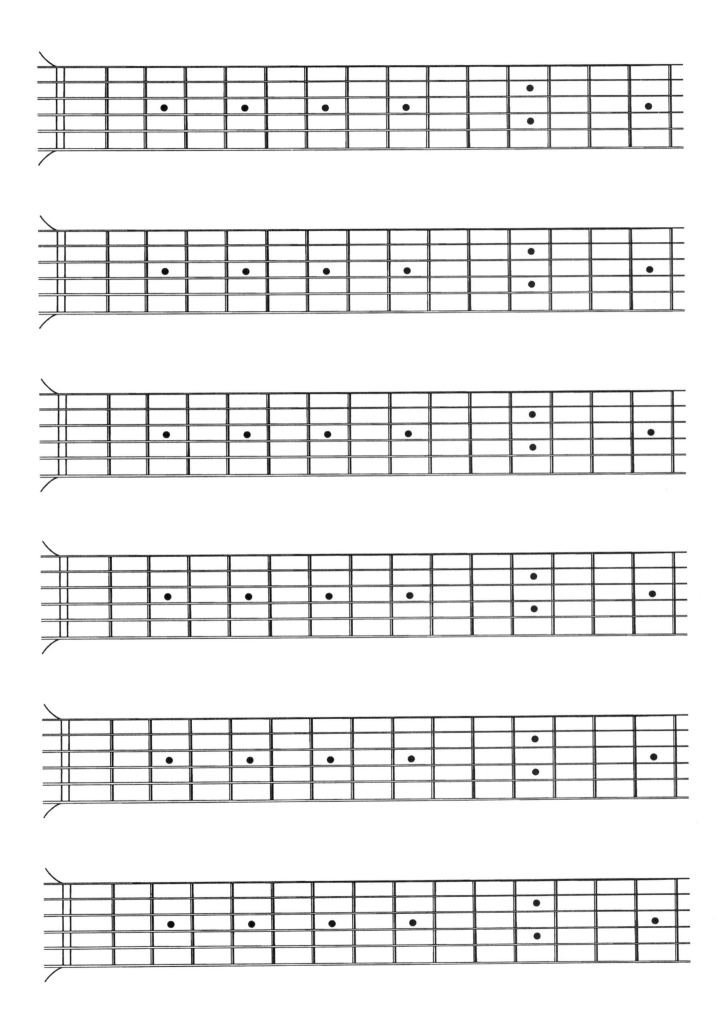

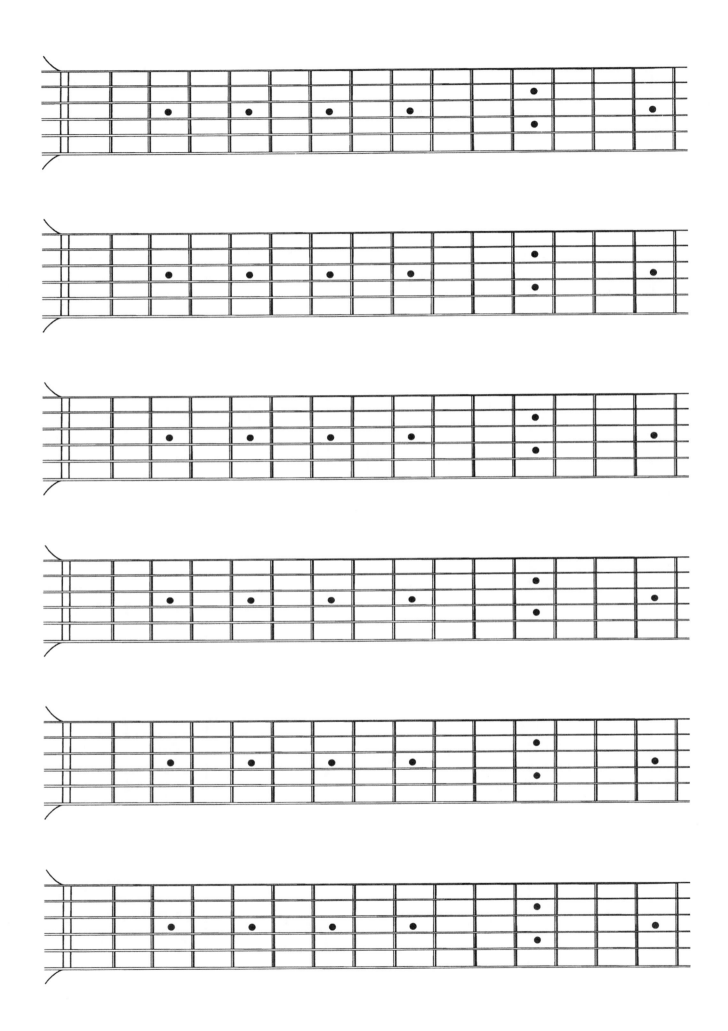

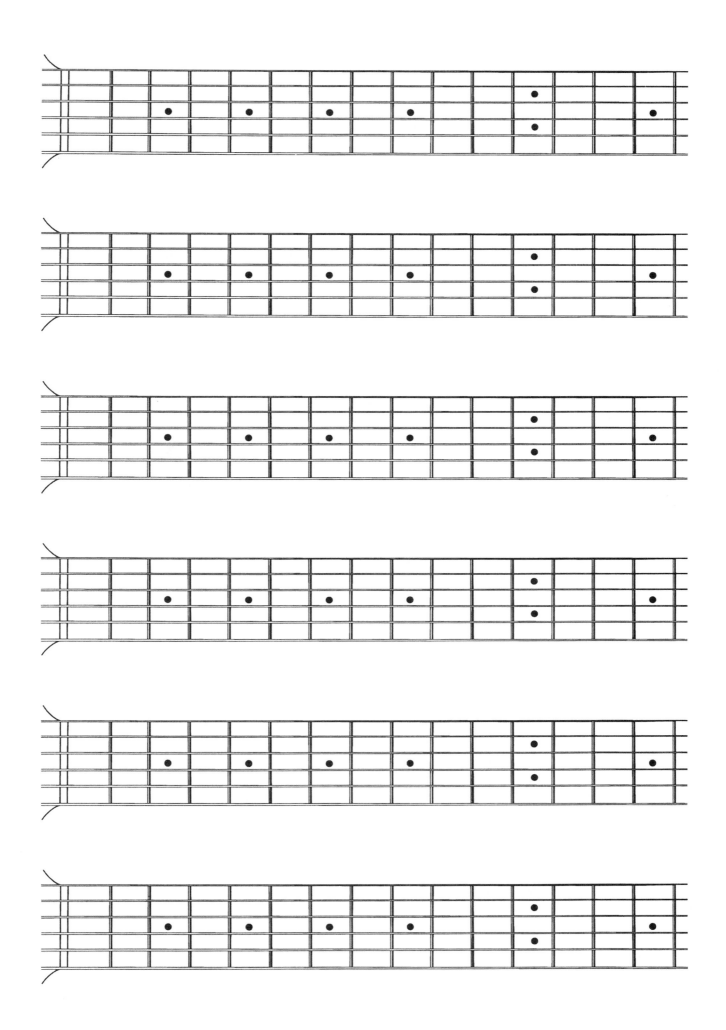

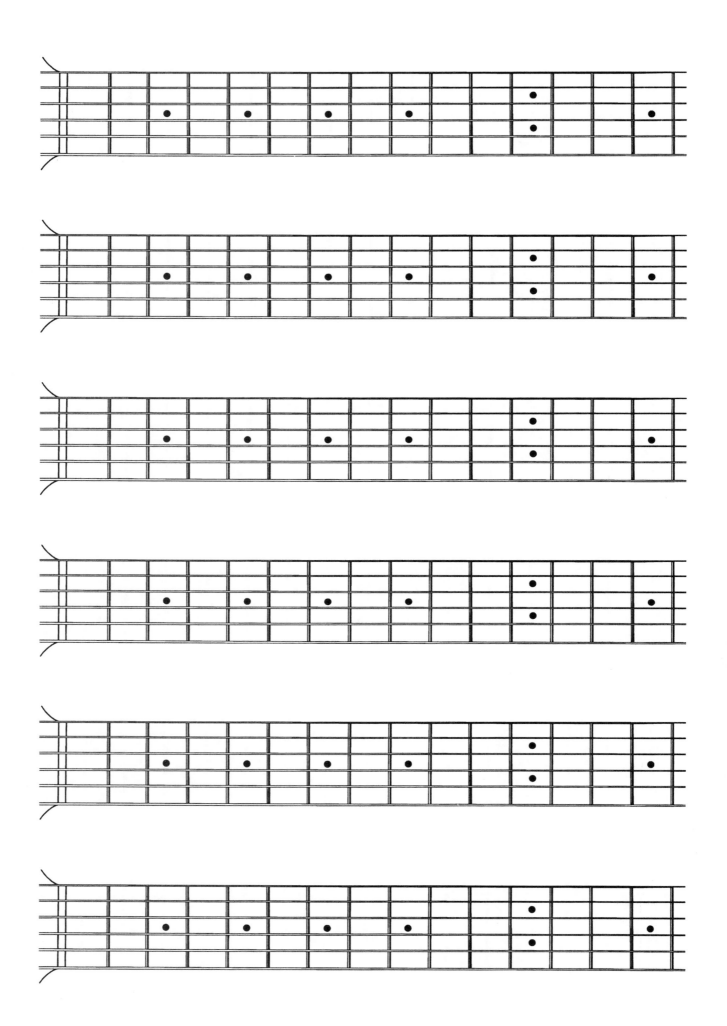

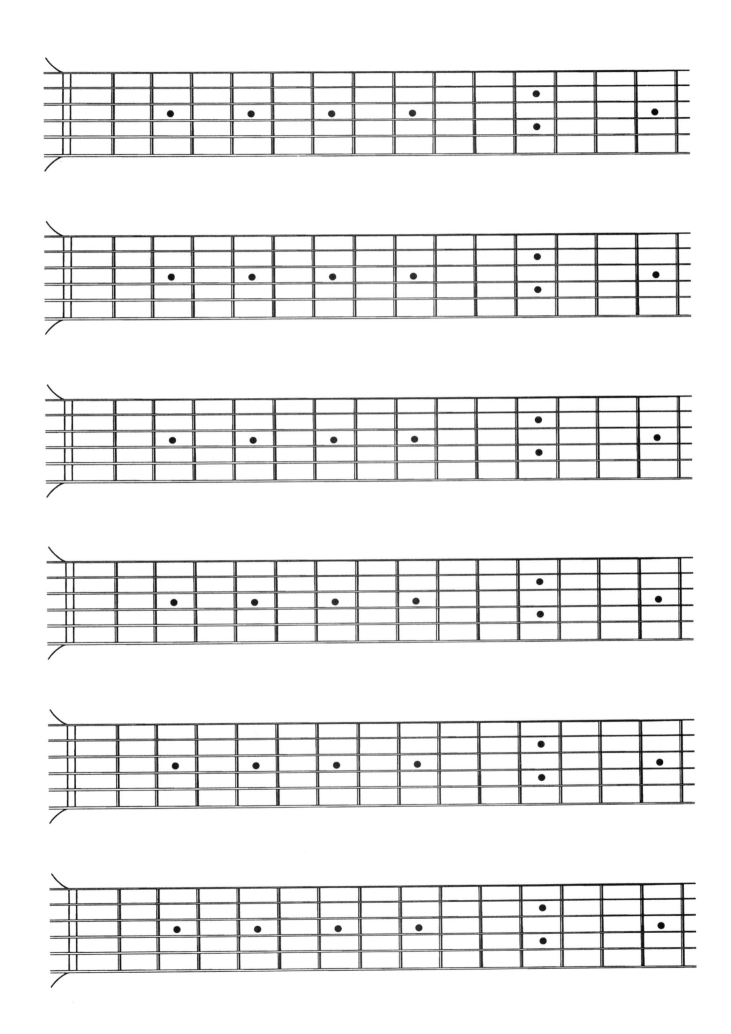

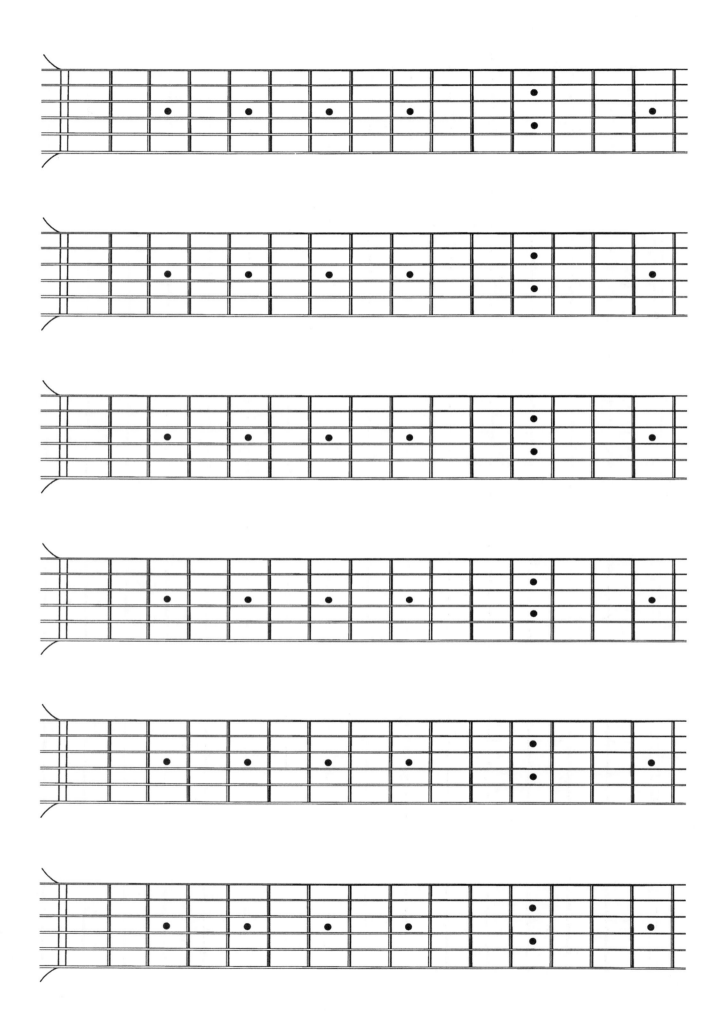

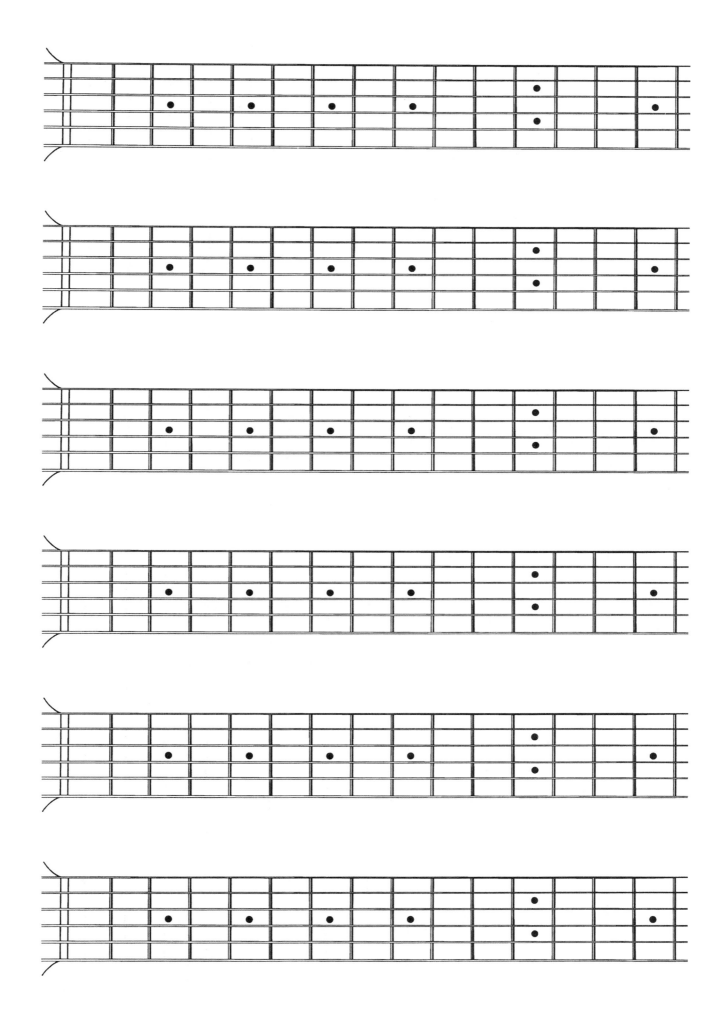

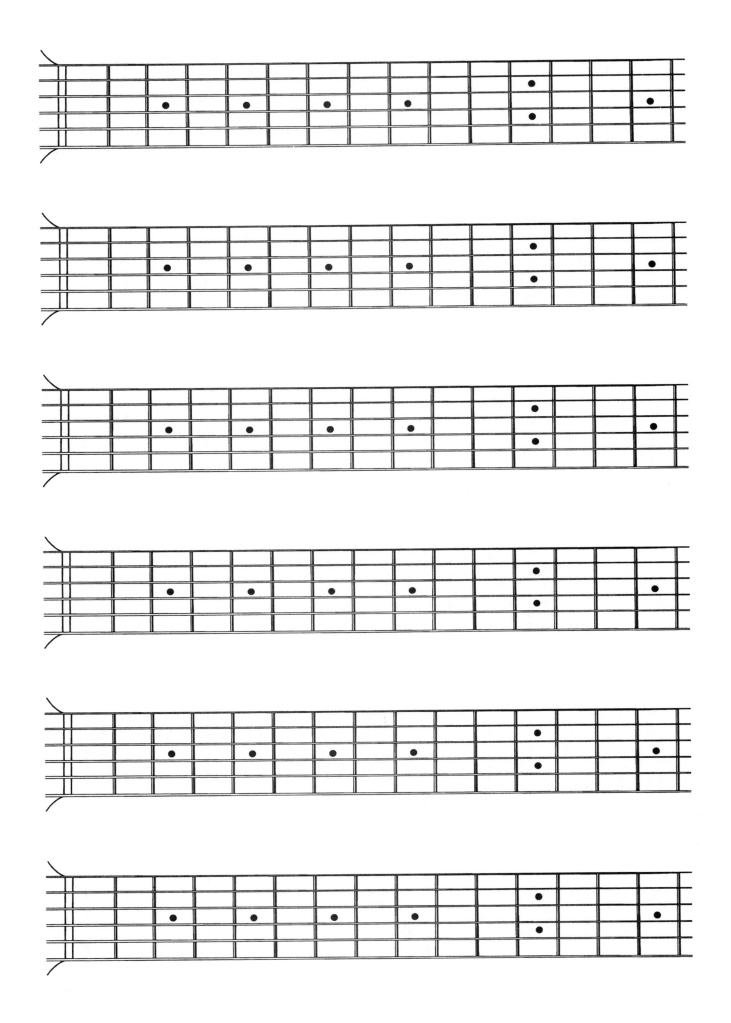

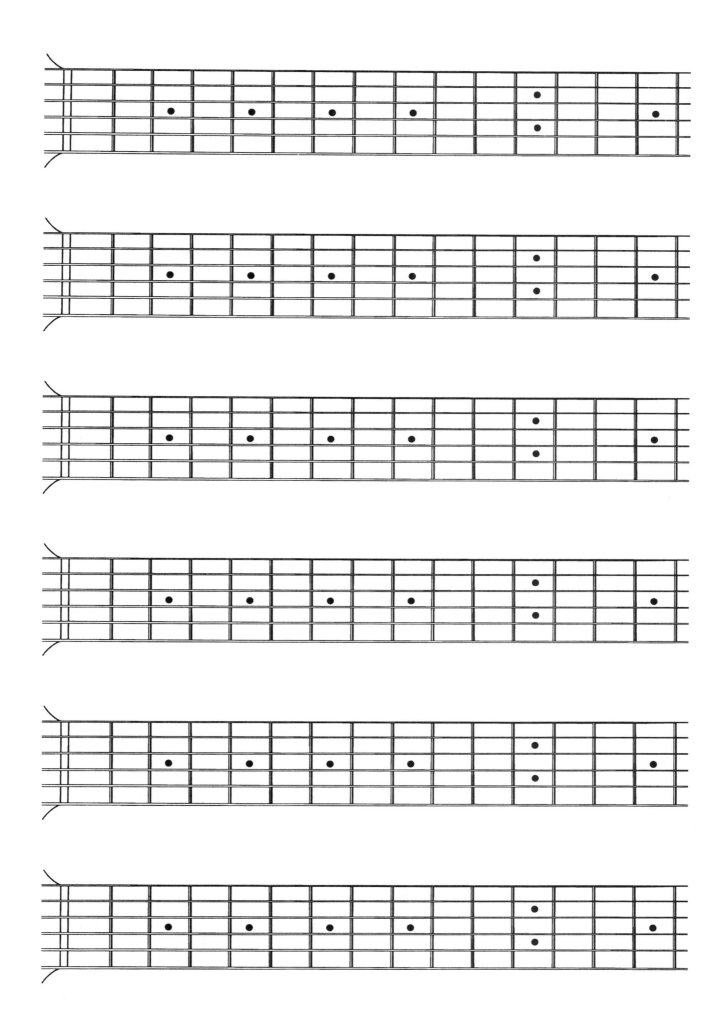

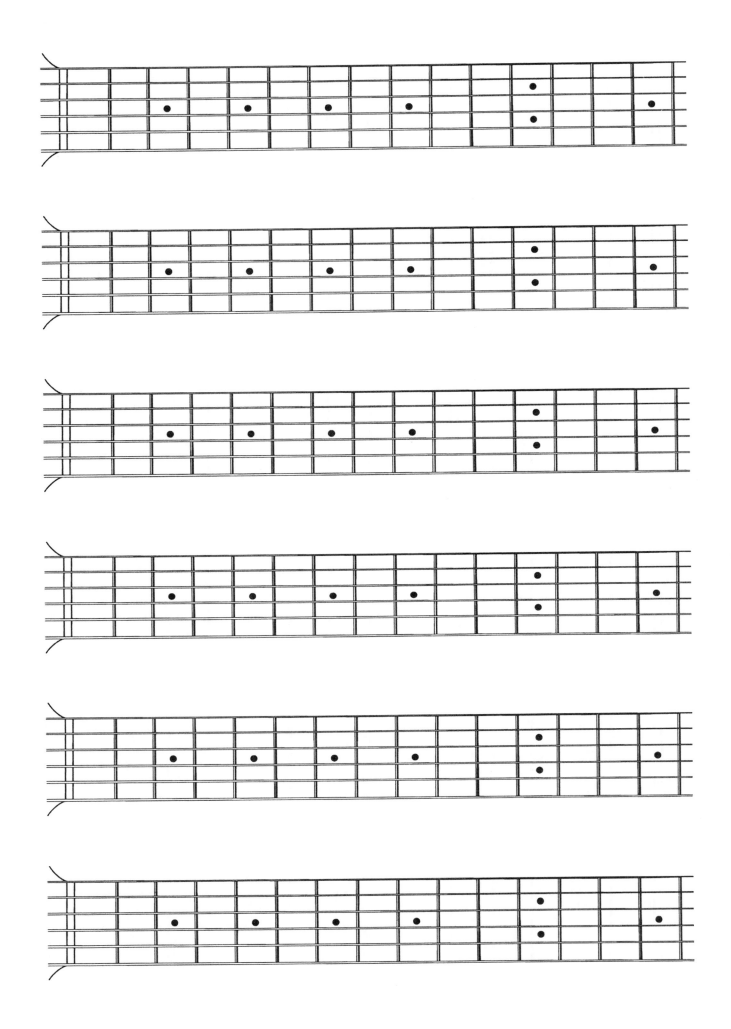

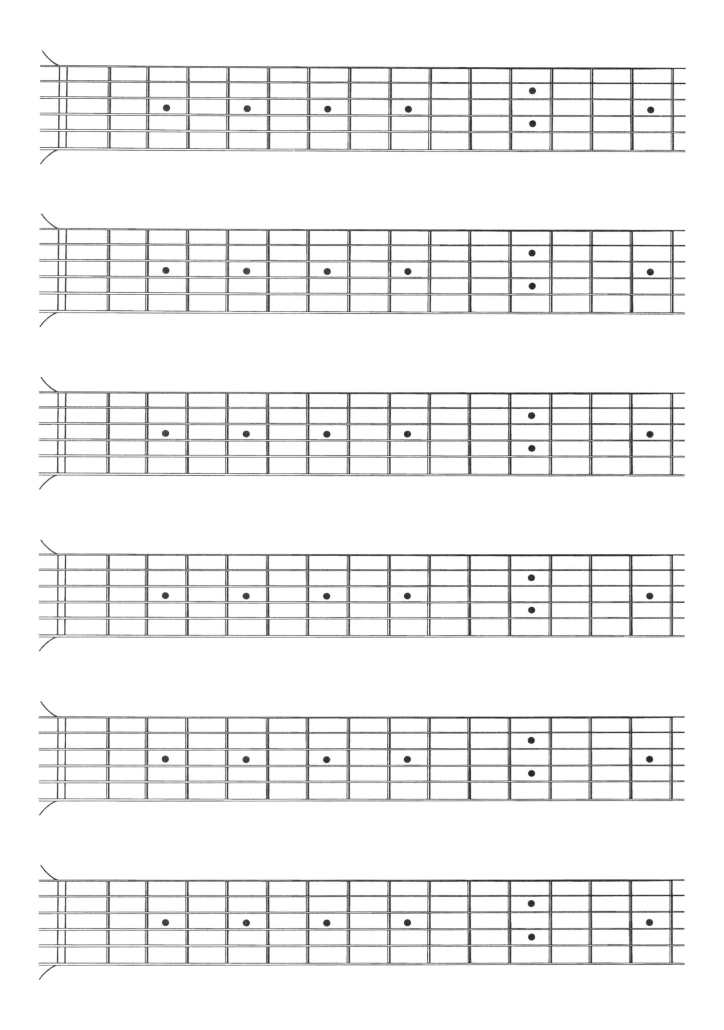

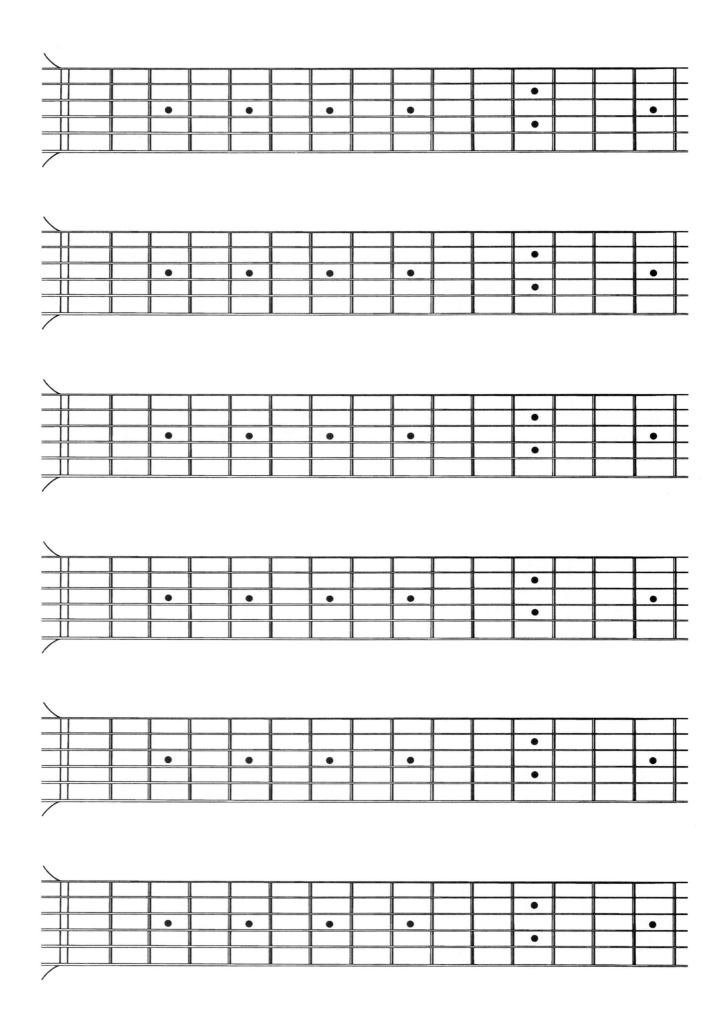

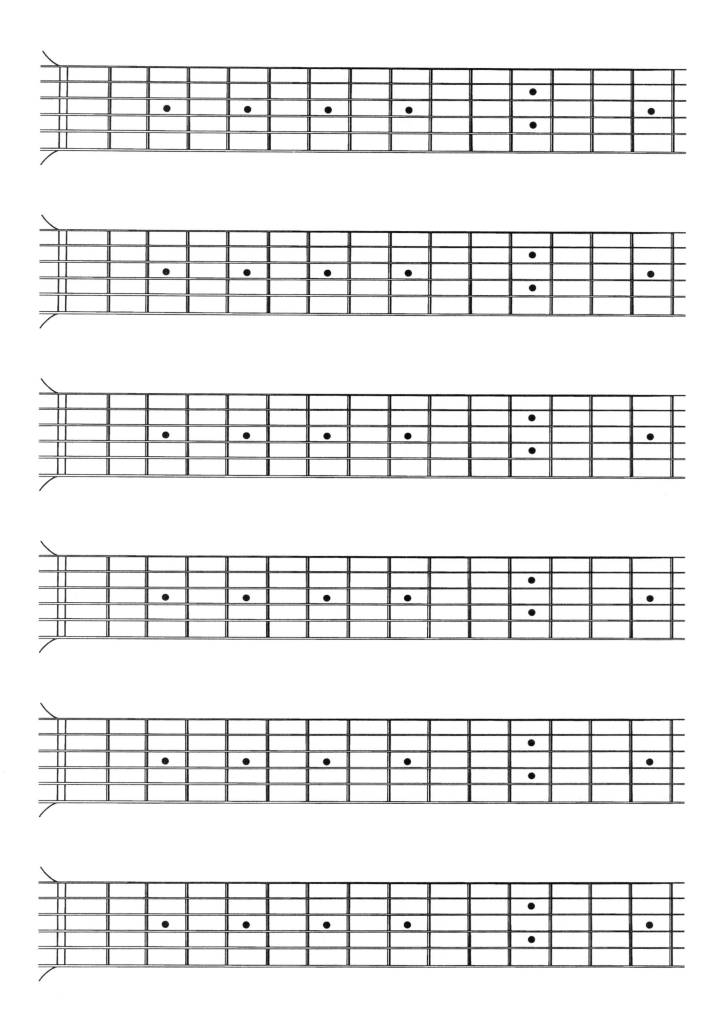

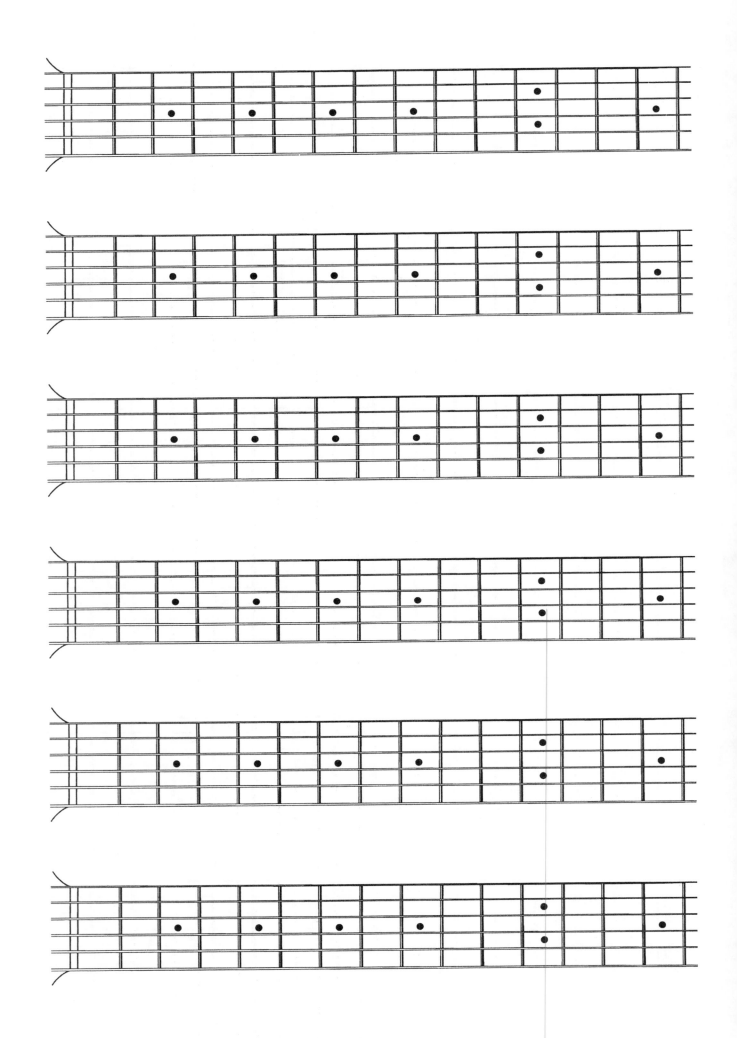

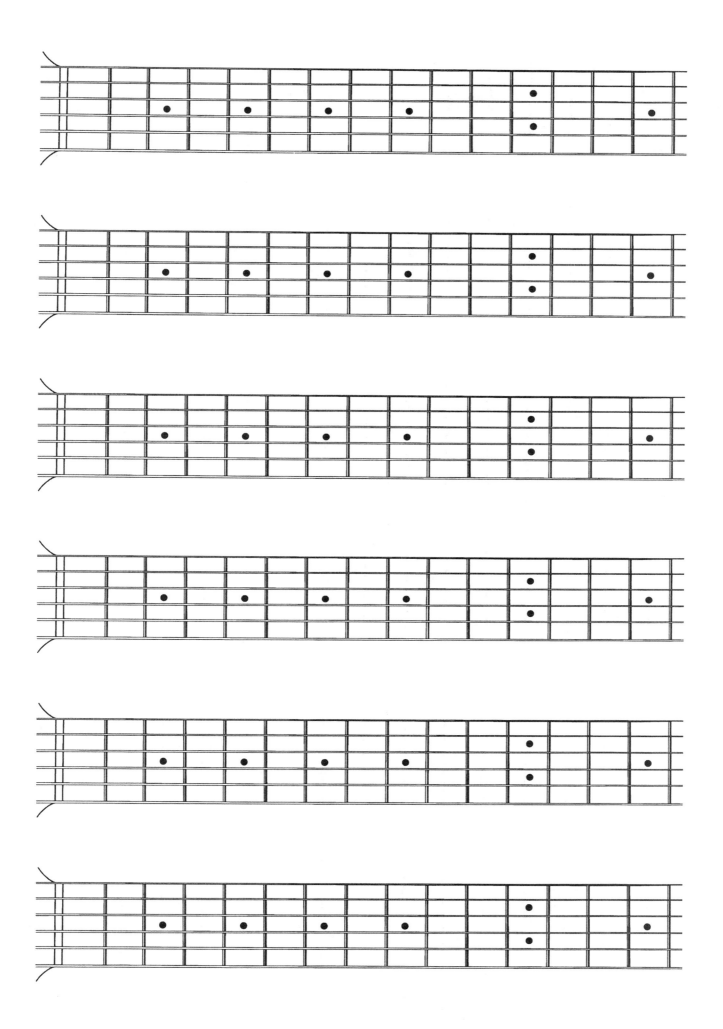

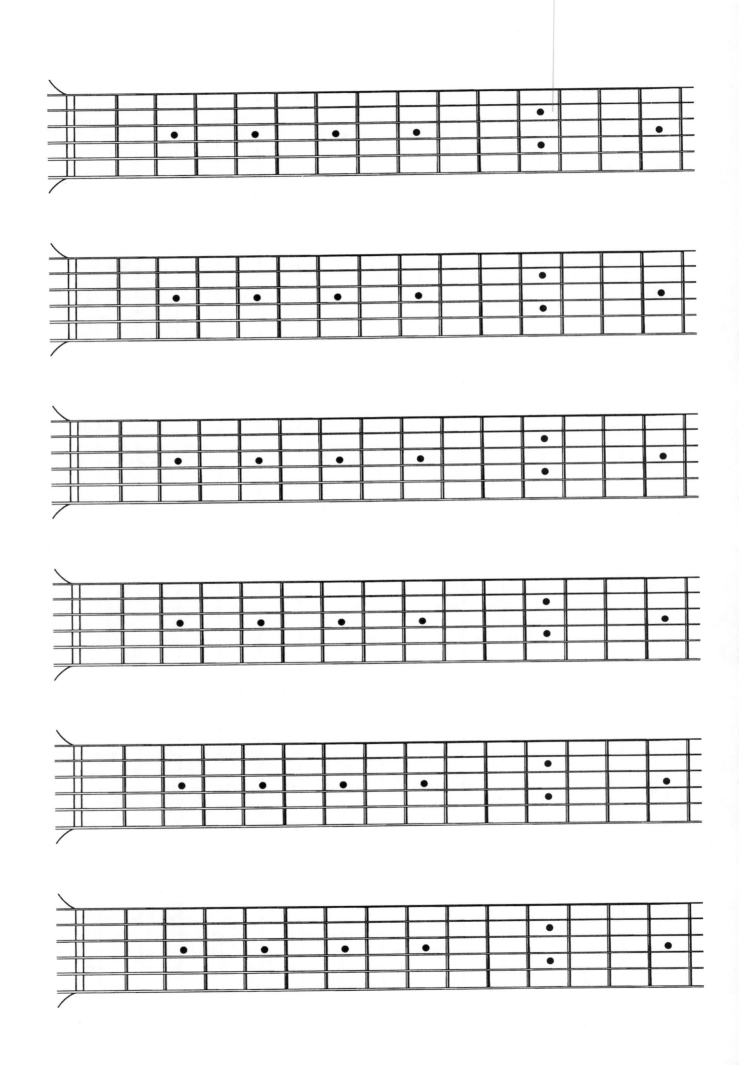

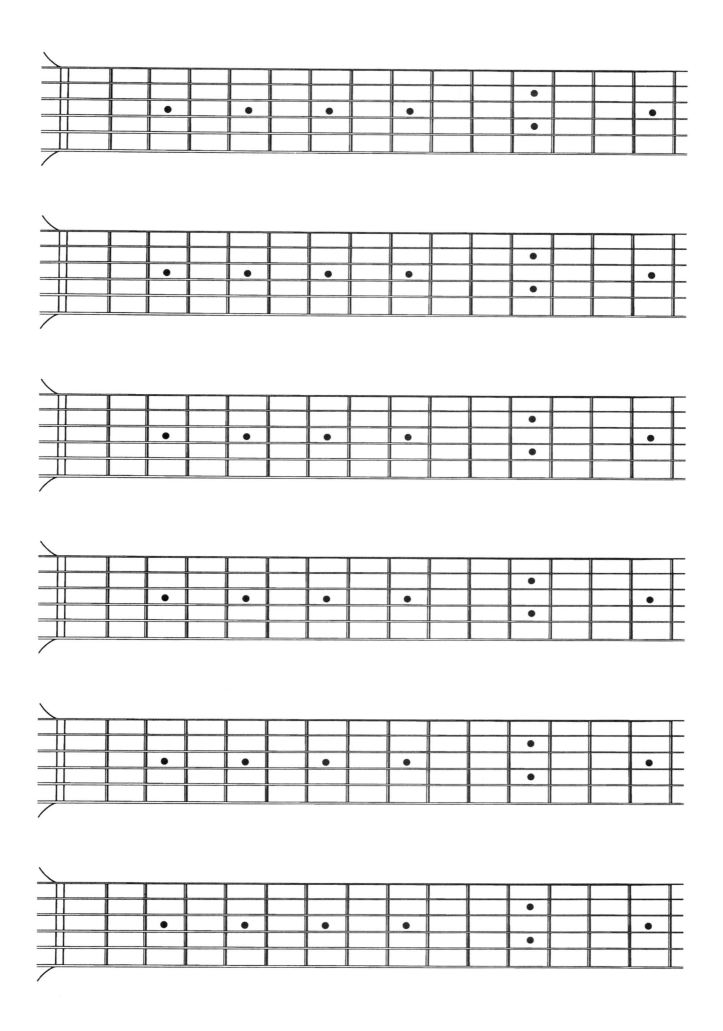

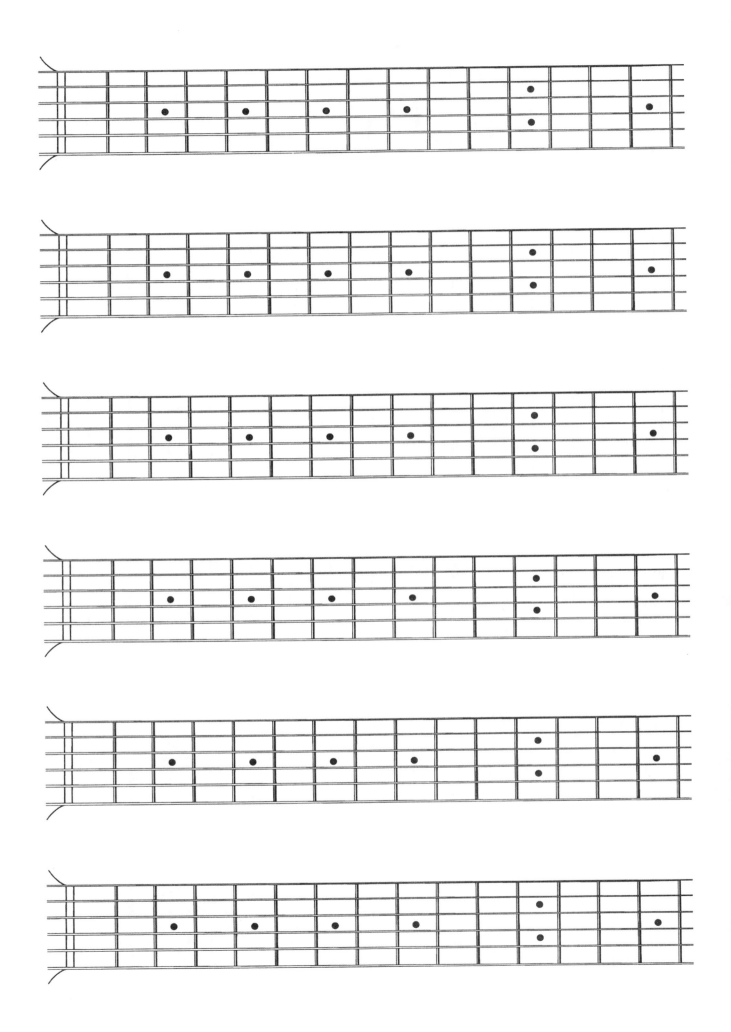

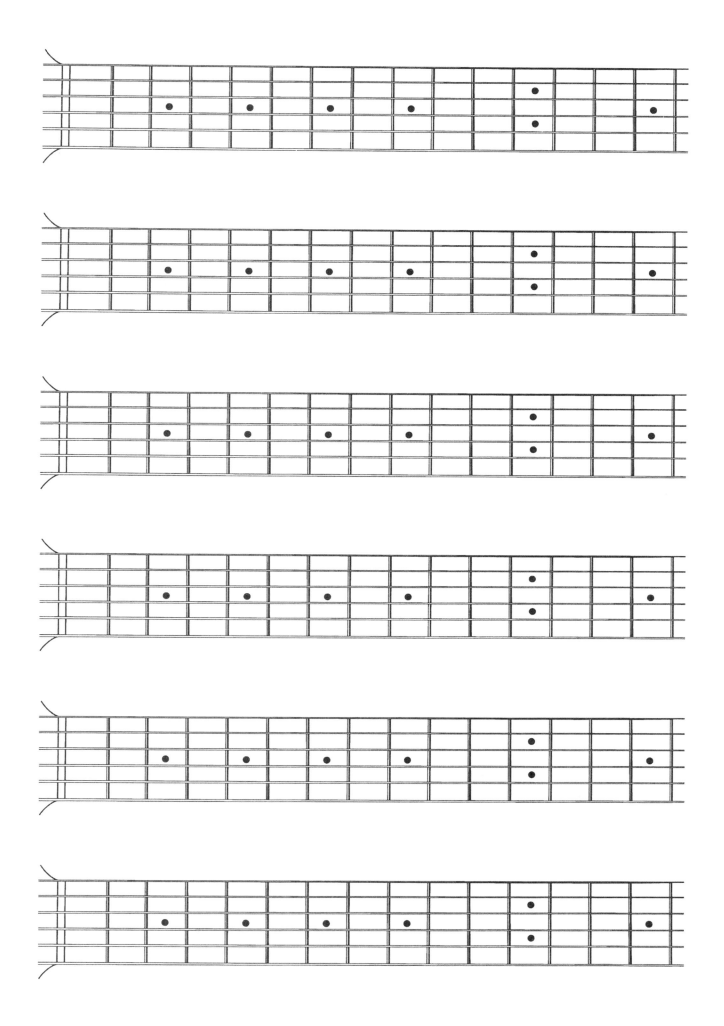

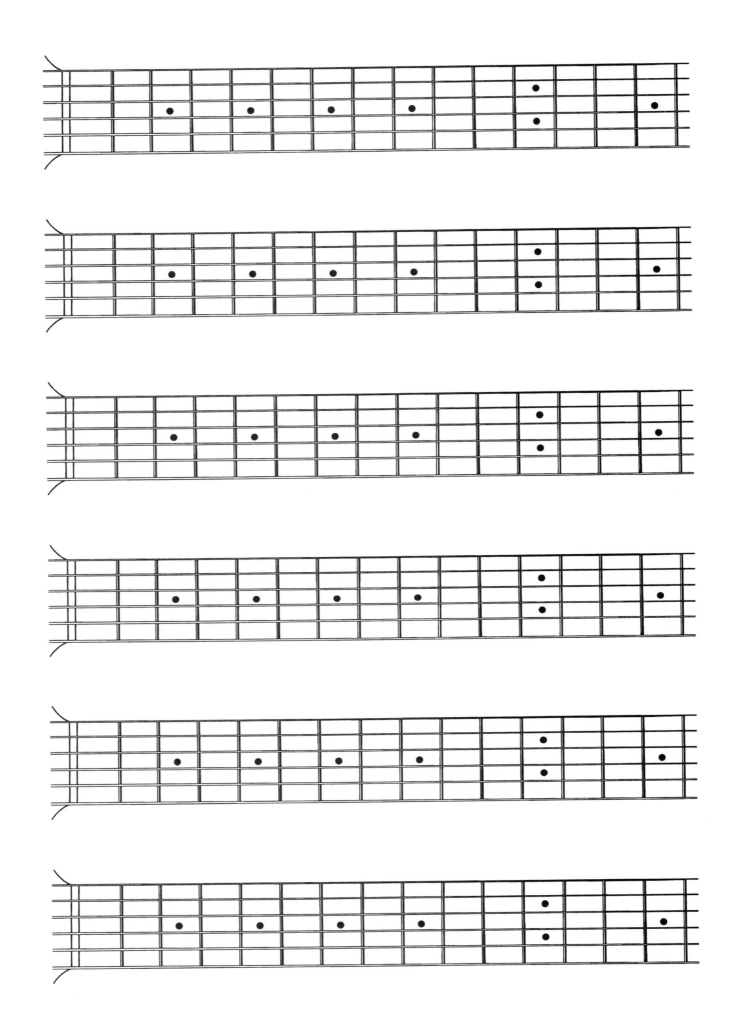

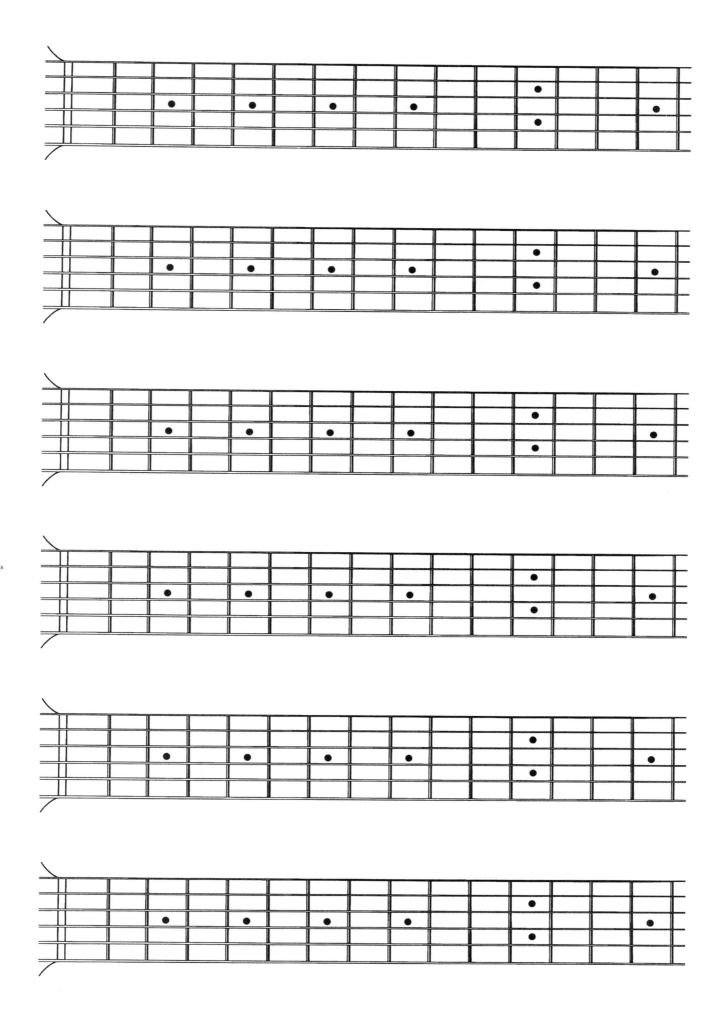

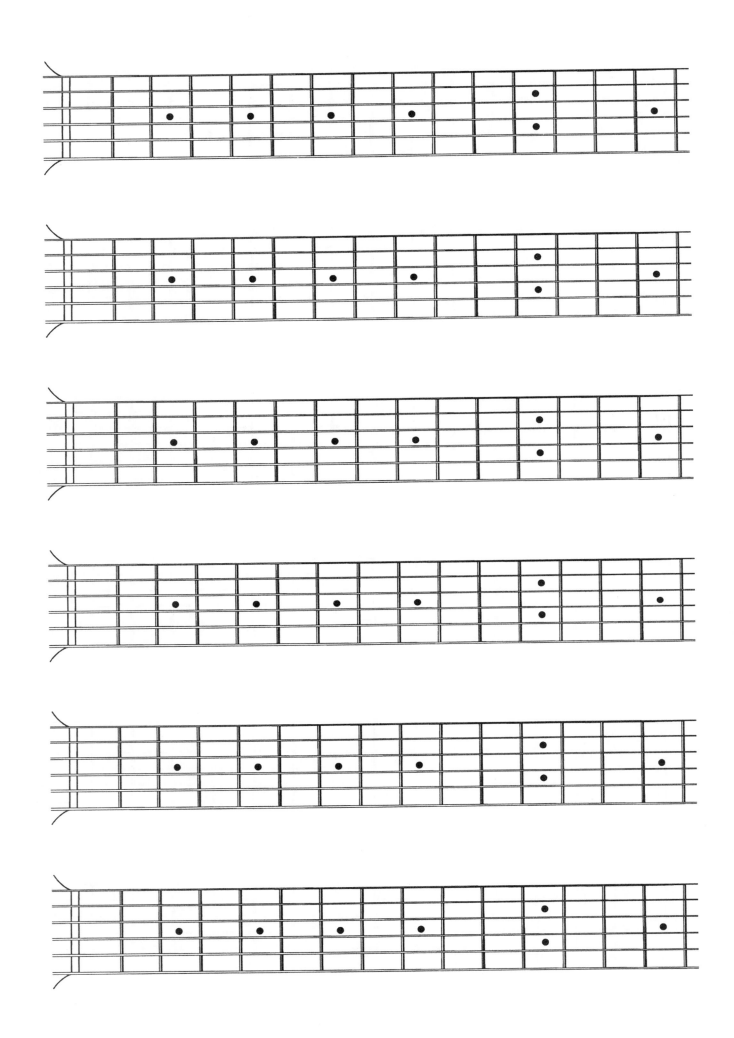

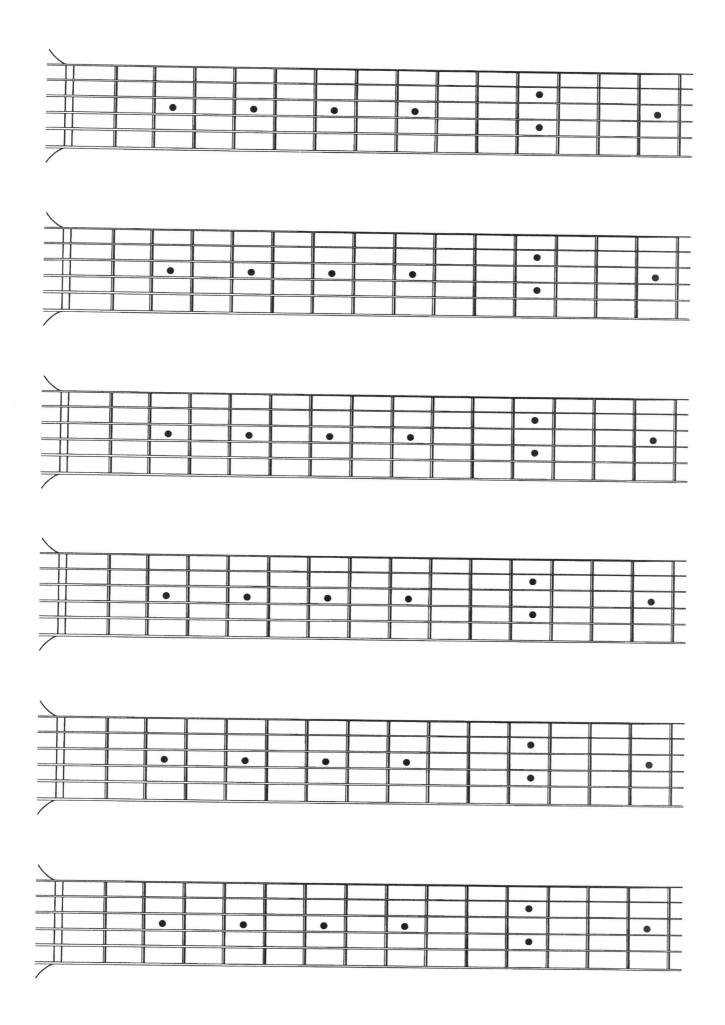

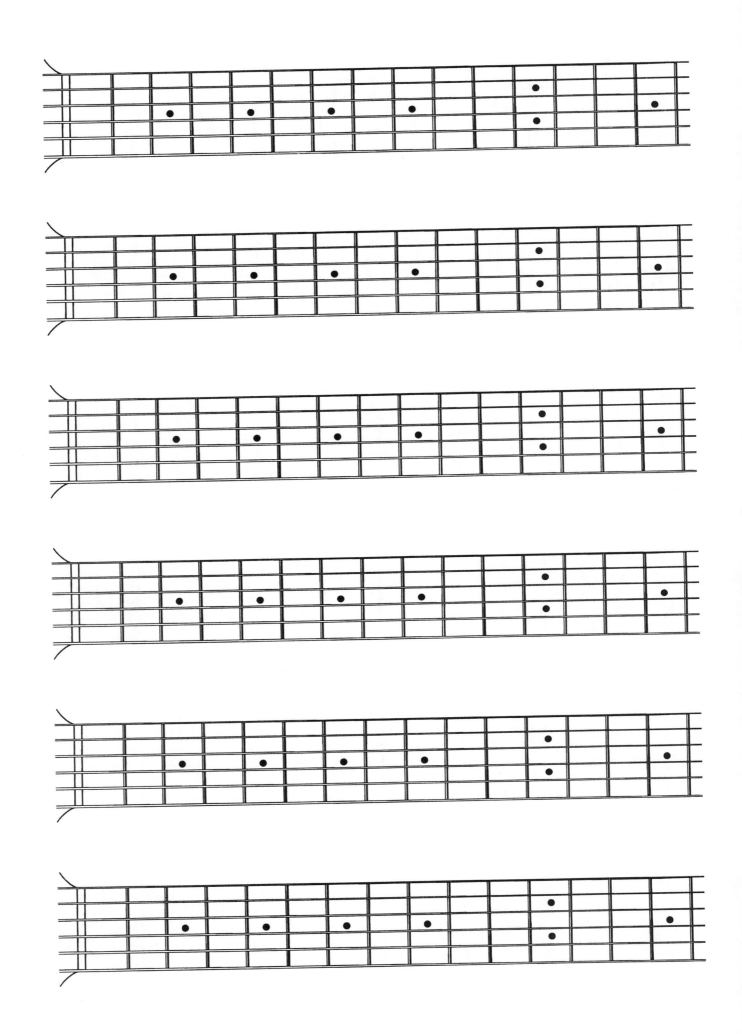

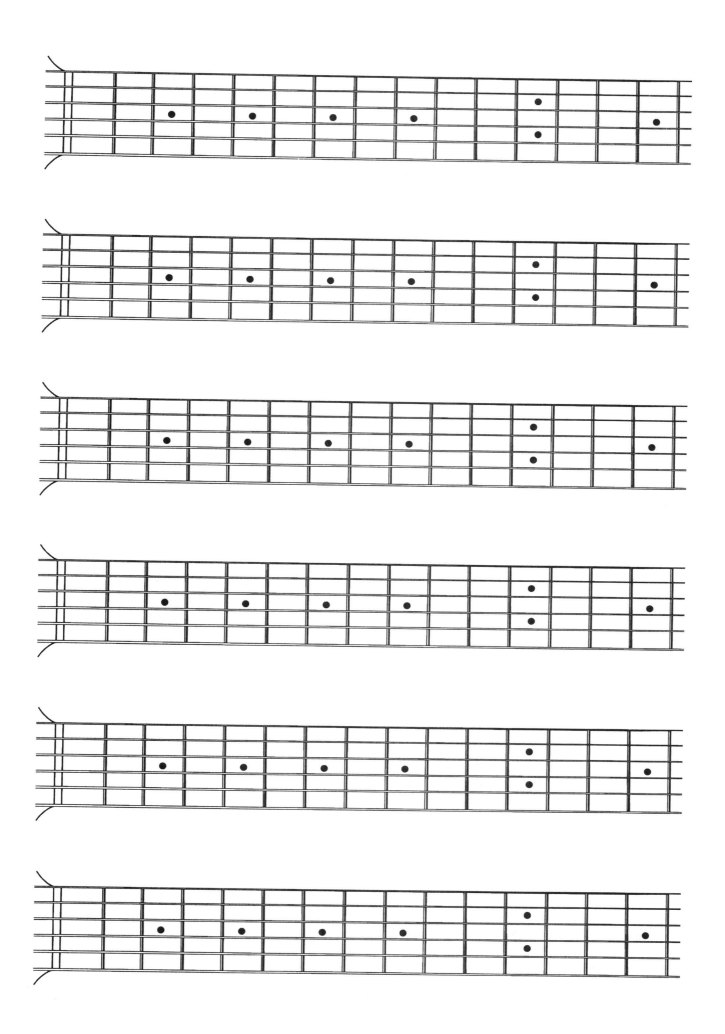

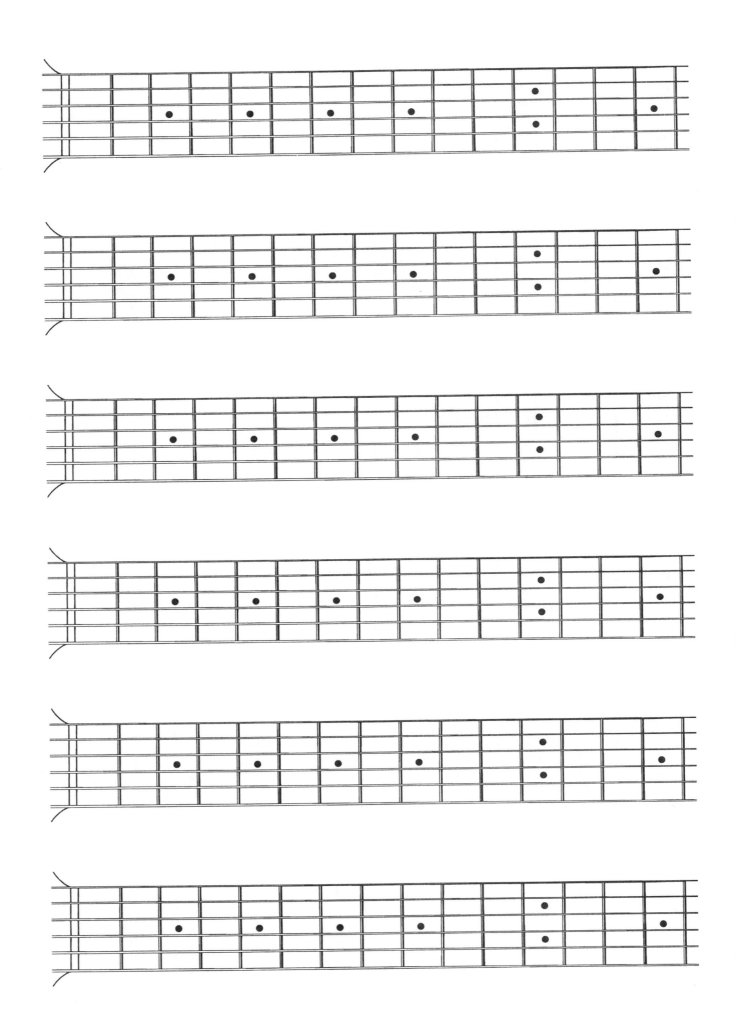

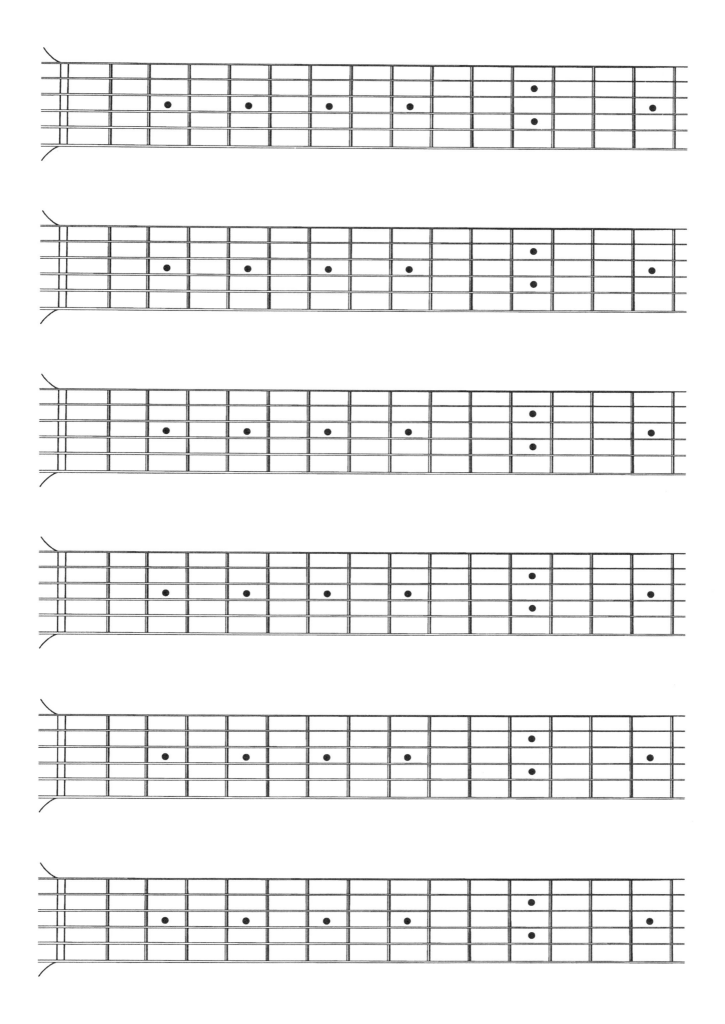

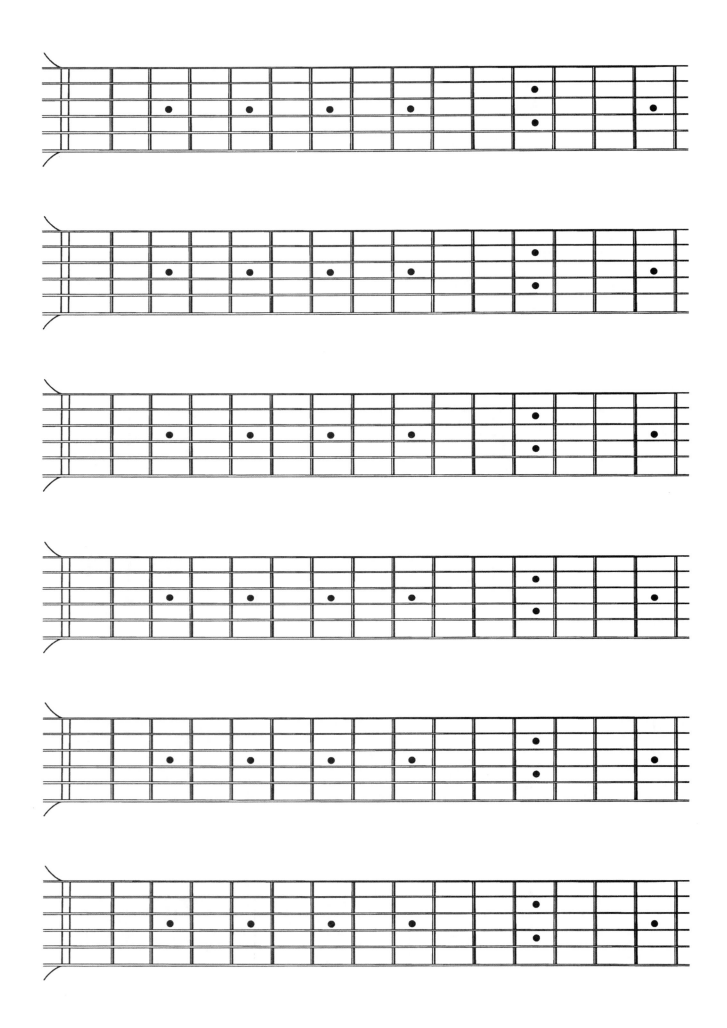

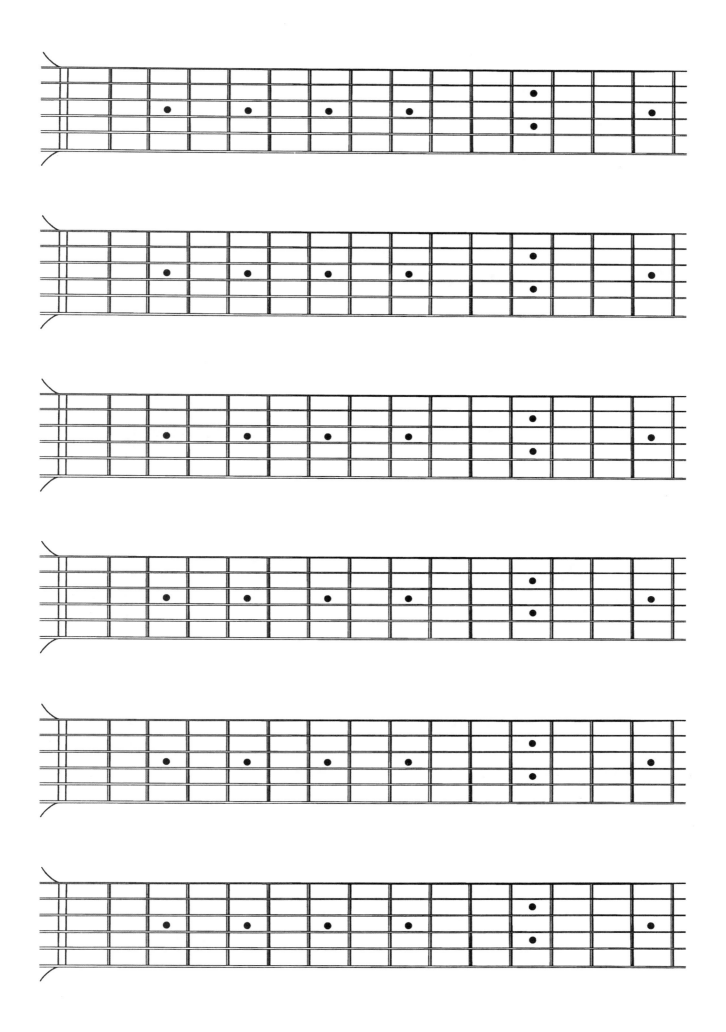

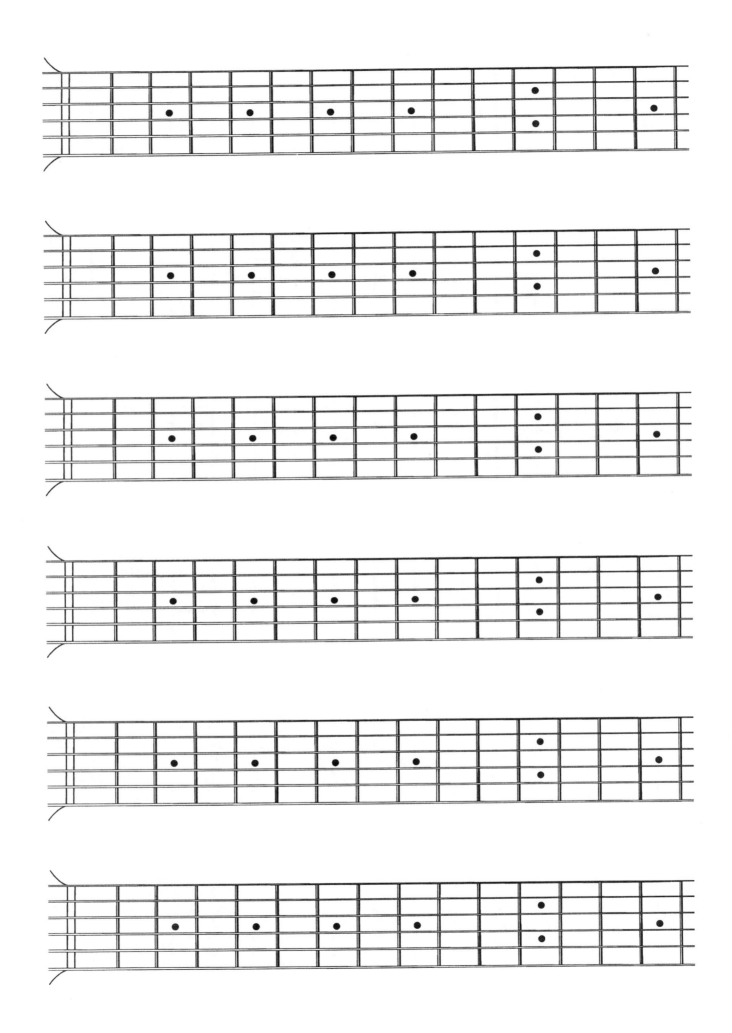

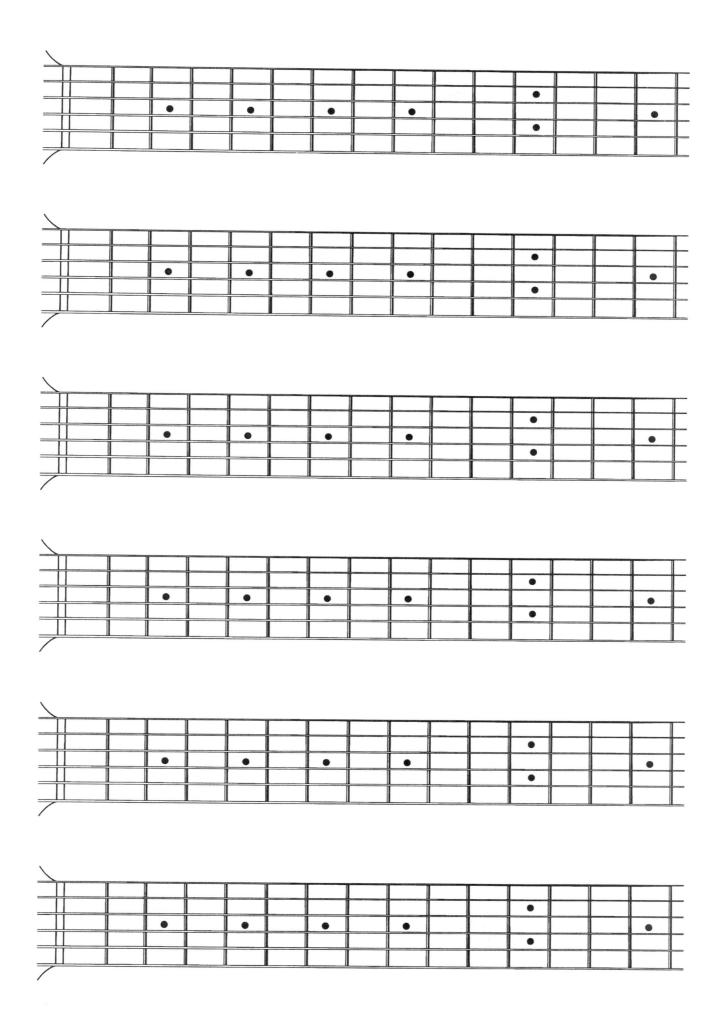

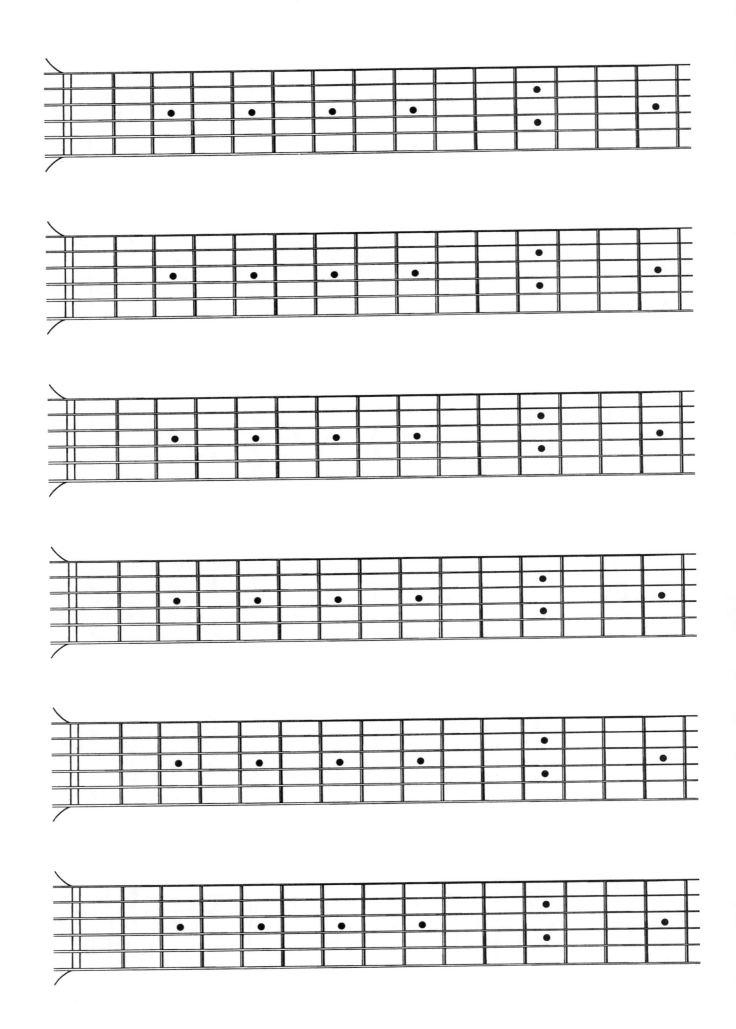

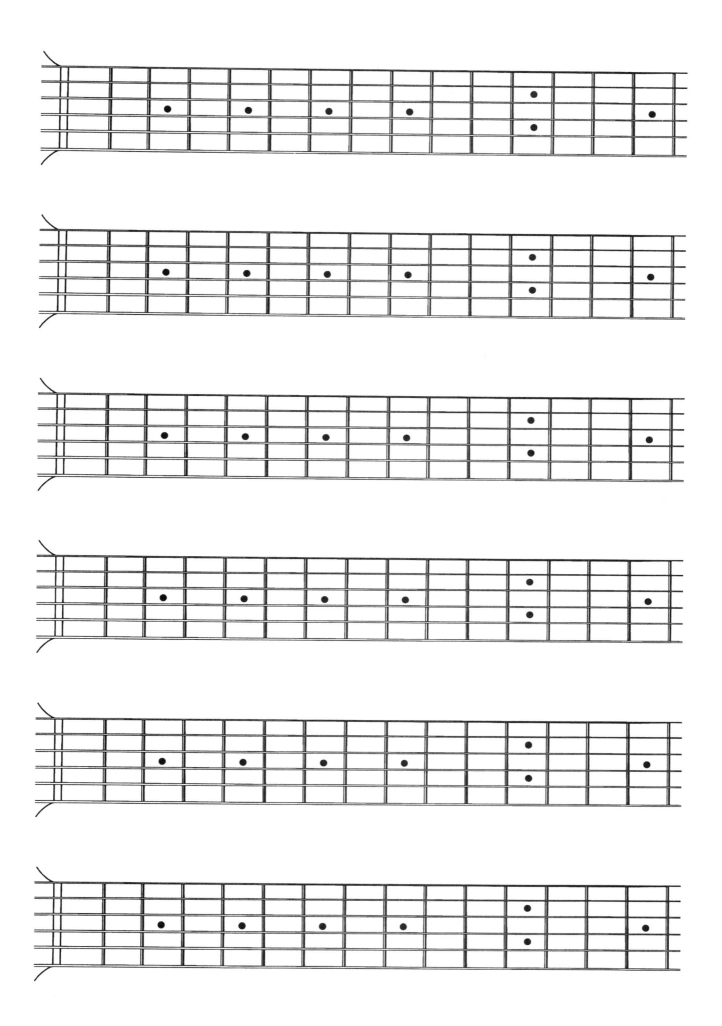

GUITAR TAB GLOSSARY **

TABLATURE EXPLANATION

READING TABLATURE: Tablature illustrates the six strings of the guitar. Notes and chords are indicated by the placement of fret numbers on a given string(s).

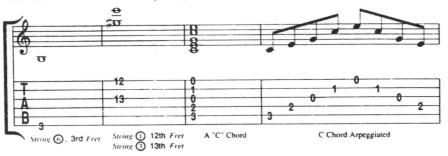

String ⑥ , 3rd Fret   String ① 12th Fret   A "C" Chord   C Chord Arpeggiated
String ③ 13th Fret

BENDING NOTES

HALF STEP: Play the note and bend string one half step.*

WHOLE STEP: Play the note and bend string one whole step.

PREBEND AND RELEASE: Bend the string, play it, then release to the original note.

RHYTHM SLASHES

STRUM INDICA-TIONS: Strum with indicated rhythm. The chord voicings are found on the first page of the transcription underneath the song title.

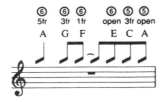

INDICATING SINGLE NOTES USING RHYTHM SLASHES: Very often single notes are incorporated into a rhythm part. The note name is indicated above the rhythm slash with a fret number and a string indication.

*A half step is the smallest interval in Western music; it is equal to one fret. A whole step equals two frets.

**By Kenn Chipkin and Aaron Stang

ARTICULATIONS

HAMMER ON: Play lower note then "hammer on" to higher note with anoth[er] finger. Only the first note is attacked.

PULL OFF: Play higher note then "pull off" to lower note with another finger. Only the first no[te] is attacked.

LEGATO SLIDE: Play note and slide to the following note. (Only first note is attacked).

PALM MUTE: The note or notes are mute[d] by the palm of the pick hand by lightly touching the string(s) near the bridge.

ACCENT: Notes or chords are to be playe[d] with added emphasis.

DOWN STROKES AND UPSTROKES Notes or chords are to be played wit[h] either a downstroke

(⊓) or upstroke (∨) of the pick[.]